From Clay to Today

The Story of Human Beginnings through Quran and Science

Saeed Rajput

Hello Young Readers!

Ever wondered where humans came from? Dive into this fun and exciting journey through time and science to learn how the Quran and modern science together tell us the story of human evolution!

This educational book is perfect for intelligent and curious children, offering a kid-friendly version of the author's detailed research work, **"The Quranic Narrative on Human Evolution."** Discover fascinating facts and awesome stories that will make you see the world in a whole new way!

Unlock the secrets of our past and understand the amazing journey of human evolution!

And if you know Urdu language, don't forget to visit the author's YouTube channel, **@QuranThi**

QURAN THINK SPACE
and hold firmly to the rope of Allah

Chapters

1: Introduction to Quran

Before we jump into all the fun stuff, let's start with some important basics. We need to learn a bit about the Quran, which has amazing stories, and to get a sneak peek into the science of how humans evolved. Scientists have discovered so many cool things about how we came to be!

Let's kick off our journey by diving into the amazing world of the Quran.

What is the Quran?

The Quran isn't just any old book—it's super special! For over 2 billion Muslims, it's like a treasure chest filled with the words of God Himself. It's like a guidebook that helps people live their best lives. Imagine it as a giant rock, holding up the building blocks of Islam, the world's fastest-growing religion!

A Blast from the Past

Picture this: way back in 7th-century Arabia, in a city called Mecca, came the final messenger of God named Muhammad. He was known as "Truthful" and "Trustworthy" by everyone. Even though he couldn't read or write, he started getting messages from God through an angel named Gabriel. These messages eventually became the Quran.

Shaping History

When the Quran showed up, it was like a superhero swooping in to save the day! Before it came along, things were pretty tough in Arabia. People were doing all sorts of not-so-nice stuff, like treating others badly and being unfair. But the Quran changed all that—it was like a magic wand, turning darkness into light and making everything better.

Making Things Right

The Quran didn't just stop at fixing stuff in Arabia; it wanted to make the whole world a better place! It talked about treating everyone with kindness and fairness, no matter who they were. Suddenly, people started looking out for each other, sharing stuff, and being nice to animals too. It was like a big family reunion, with everyone getting along!

What's the Point?

So, why does the Quran exist? Well, it's here to help us out! It's like having a wise elder giving us advice on how to live our lives. It tells us what's good to do and what's not so good, like being honest and kind to others. Plus, it promises us a happy ending if we stick to the good stuff!

An Epic Tale

The Quran isn't just a bunch of words—it's like a storybook, but way cooler! It's written in a way that's easy to remember, so people all over the world have it memorized. And here's the coolest part: even though lots of people have tried, nobody's been able to write anything else like it! It's like a one-of-a-kind masterpiece that'll never be topped.

So, there you have it—the Quran is like a magical guidebook, a superhero story, and a wise old friend all rolled into one! It's here to help us be the best versions of ourselves and make the world a brighter place. Let's dive in and discover all the amazing secrets it holds!

Scientific Wonders in the Quran

Young explorers! Get ready to uncover some amazing scientific secrets hidden within the pages of the Quran.

What's the Deal with Science?

So, the Quran isn't exactly a science book, but guess what? It talks about some pretty cool stuff that lines up with what scientists have discovered! It's like a treasure map leading us to amazing discoveries.

Water: The Source of Life

In the Quran, it says that everything living came from water. Isn't that fascinating? Scientists have found out that our bodies are mostly made of water too! It's like we're all water buddies!

The Big Bang Theory: The Beginning of Everything

Imagine this: the Quran talks about how the heavens and the earth used to be stuck together, and then they got separated. That's kind of like what scientists say about the Big Bang! It's like the universe started with a big explosion and then everything spread out.

Embryology: The Miracle of Life

The Quran describes how humans start from a tiny drop and then grow into babies. Isn't that incredible? Even though scientists didn't know much about how babies develop back then, the Quran got it right!

Iron: A Gift from the Stars

Did you know that iron didn't come from Earth originally? Scientists think it came from outer space in meteorites! The Quran knew about this way before scientists did—it's like it had insider knowledge!

Meeting of the Seas: Nature's Boundaries

When two seas meet, there's a special barrier that keeps them separate. It's like they each have their own space! Scientists have found out about this barrier too, showing how the Quran knows all about nature's secrets.

Heavenly Orbits: Celestial Moves

The Quran talks about how the sun, the moon, and all the stars move in orbits. Scientists used to think everything in space was still, but now we know they're all moving around! It's like the Quran knew the universe's secret moves!

Mountains as Stakes: Earth's Hidden Strength

In the Quran, it says mountains are like stakes holding the Earth together. Guess what? Scientists have found out that mountains have deep roots underground, just like big nails holding up a tent!

Expansion of the Universe: The Growing Cosmos

The Quran says that God keeps expanding the heavens. Scientists didn't know about this until the 20th century when they discovered that the universe is getting bigger all the time!

Pain Receptors: Feeling the Burn

Even though people used to think our brains felt pain, the Quran talks about how we feel pain through our skin. Scientists found out that our skin has special pain sensors, just like the Quran said!

Fingerprints: Nature's Signature

The Quran says that everyone's fingerprints are unique. Scientists only figured this out a few hundred years ago, but the Quran knew it all along! It's like our fingerprints are our own special stamps.

Let's Keep Exploring!

Isn't it amazing how the Quran knew all this cool stuff way before scientists did? It's like a magical book full of secrets waiting to be discovered! Let's keep exploring and uncover even more wonders together!

2: Introduction to Science of Human Evolution

Let's explore the Science of Human Evolution

Imagine a fascinating journey that started millions of years ago and led to us, the humans, living in the world today! This journey is the story of human evolution, and it's filled with amazing discoveries and incredible beings.

Lamarckism

Have you ever heard of giraffes and their long necks? Well, a long time ago, a scientist named Jean-Baptiste Lamarck had an interesting idea about how giraffes got their long necks. He thought that giraffes stretched their necks to reach high leaves on trees, and this stretching made their necks longer over time. Lamarck believed that traits like this could be passed down to their babies. However, modern science has found out that Lamarck's ideas were not quite right.

Darwinism

Now, let's talk about a famous scientist named Charles Darwin. He went on a big adventure on a ship called the HMS Beagle. Darwin noticed that animals in different places had different traits. For example, he saw tortoises with different shells on the Galápagos Islands. Some had shells that were good for eating low plants, while others had shells perfect for reaching high plants.

Darwin came up with a brilliant idea called natural selection. This means that animals with traits that help them survive in their environment are more likely to live longer and have babies. Over many, many years, these traits become more common in a population, and that's how species change over time. Darwin's ideas changed the way we understand life on Earth forever!

Neo-Darwinism

Later on, scientists combined Darwin's ideas with another scientist's work named Gregor Mendel. They found out that traits are passed down through tiny units called genes. This helped us understand how species change over many generations. Isn't that cool?

Punctuated Equilibrium

Imagine if some animals stayed the same for a long time and then changed quickly. That's what punctuated equilibrium is all about! It's like a burst of change after a long time of staying the same. Scientists have found evidence of this happening with certain creatures in the fossil record.

Creationism

Some people believe that a powerful being created all living things. This idea is called creationism. It's based on religious stories that explain how everything came to be. There are different versions of creationism, like Young Earth Creationism, which says everything happened in a short time, and Old Earth Creationism, which allows for a longer process.

Intelligent Design

Another idea is called Intelligent Design. It suggests that some things in nature are too complex to have happened by chance. Instead, they believe that someone very smart must have designed them. While this idea is debated, it's important to know that science and religion can have different ways of explaining things.

Genetics and Evolution

Did you know that our genes hold clues to our past? Scientists study how traits are passed down from parents to children, and this helps them understand how species change over time. It's like a genetic puzzle that helps us piece together the story of life on Earth!

Let's Sum Up!

So, there you have it! The story of human evolution is like a puzzle with many pieces. Scientists use evidence from fossils, genes, and observations to understand how life has changed over millions of years. Isn't it amazing to think about how far we've come? Keep exploring, and who knows? Maybe one day you'll make a discovery that changes the world too!

Let's Explore the Taxonomy of Human Evolution!

Taxonomy is like a big family tree that helps scientists organize and understand how living things are related to each other. When it comes to humans and our evolutionary journey, taxonomy plays a key role in discovering the complex web of relationships between different species.

The Big Picture: Domain to Species

Taxonomy starts with the broadest categories and goes down to the most specific. For humans, it looks something like this:

- **Domain:** Eukarya

- **Kingdom:** Animalia

- **Phylum:** Chordata

- **Subphylum:** Vertebrata

- **Class:** Mammalia

- **Order:** Primates

- **Family:** Hominidae

- **Genus:** Homo

- **Species:** Homo sapiens

Now, let's break down what each of these levels means for understanding human evolution.

Exploring the Levels

- **Domain (Eukarya):** Imagine this as the biggest category, like a giant umbrella covering all organisms with complex cells. We're in this domain because we have cells with nuclei, just like plants and animals.

- **Kingdom (Animalia):** Within the Eukarya domain, we belong to the Animalia kingdom. This group includes creatures that can move around and munch on other organisms for food. It's where the action happens!

- **Phylum (Chordata):** Now, we zoom in a bit. In the Animalia kingdom, humans belong to the Chordata phylum. These are animals with a special flexible rod called a notochord running down their back. In us, that notochord becomes our backbone!

- **Subphylum (Vertebrata):** Within the Chordata phylum, we're in the Vertebrata subphylum. This means we have a cool backbone made of bones protecting our precious spinal cord. It's like our body's superhero cape!

- **Class (Mammalia):** Here's where things get cosy. We're in the Mammalia class, which includes warm-blooded animals with hair or fur. Most of us mammals give birth to live babies and feed them with milk from special glands. It's all about cuddly warmth!

- **Order (Primates):** Moving along, humans are part of the Primate order. This group includes our close relatives like monkeys, apes, and lemurs. We're known for our dexterous hands and forward-facing eyes, perfect for exploring and socializing!

- **Family (Hominidae):** Hold onto your hats, because here's where the family reunion gets exciting! We belong to the Hominidae family, which includes amazing creatures like gorillas, chimpanzees, bonobos, orangutans, and, drumroll please... humans!

- **Genus (Homo):** Now, let's zoom in even closer. Humans are classified in the Homo genus, along with other extinct human species like Neanderthals and Denisovans. It's like a club of ancient relatives, each with its own story to tell.

- **Species (Homo sapiens):** And finally, we arrive at our species name, Homo sapiens. "Homo" refers to our genus, and "sapiens" means wise or intelligent. It's what makes us unique as the smart cookies of the Homo club, the only surviving species of humans on the block.

Why It Matters

Understanding the taxonomy of human evolution isn't just about memorizing names and categories; it's like uncovering clues to a grand mystery—the story of our past and our connection to all living beings. By piecing together this puzzle, we gain insight into our ancestral history and grasp how we've evolved into the incredible creatures we are today!

The Ever-Changing Field

Taxonomy isn't set in stone; it evolves just like the species it classifies. As scientists make new discoveries and develop better tools for studying evolution, our understanding of taxonomy grows and changes too. It's a dynamic field that's always expanding our knowledge of life on Earth!

Journey into the World of Fossil Discoveries

Imagine if rocks could speak, what stories would they tell? Well, that's precisely what fossils do! They're like ancient clues left behind by plants, animals, and even tiny microbes, giving us a glimpse into the distant past.

Fossils: Windows to the Past

Fossils are the amazing remains or traces of ancient life that have been preserved in rocks for millions of years. They come in all shapes and sizes, from bones and teeth to imprints and petrified wood. These ancient treasures hold valuable information about extinct species, their behaviours, and the environments they lived in.

Imagine finding a dinosaur bone or a fossilized leaf—it's like holding a piece of history in your hands! Each fossil tells a story, helping scientists to piece together the puzzle of life long before humans roamed the Earth. By studying fossils, we can learn about how creatures lived, what they ate, and how they adapted to their surroundings. It's a fascinating glimpse into the distant past, showing us the incredible diversity of life that once thrived on our planet.

Creating a Fossil: Nature's Time Capsule

Creating a fossil is no easy feat; it takes just the right conditions. First, the remains of an organism need to be protected from scavengers and decay. This usually happens when the remains get buried quickly, like under a sudden landslide or at the bottom of a body of water.

Next, the buried remains get covered by layers of sediment, like sand or mud. Over time, more and more layers, pile on top, pressing down and turning everything into rock. This process can take millions of years!

Meanwhile, minerals from water seep into the bones or other hard parts of the organism. These minerals slowly replace the original material, turning the remains into stone. It's like nature's way of making a time capsule, preserving ancient life for us to discover and study millions of years later.

Let's Dig into Some Fossil Finds!

Hold onto your hats, because we're about to uncover some seriously awesome fossils:

- **Graecopithecus (Greece & Bulgaria, 7 Million Years Old):** Imagine stumbling upon a jawbone that could rewrite history! That's what happened in Greece in 1944. This ancient jawbone might just be a distant cousin of ours, but the debate is still raging!

- **Sahelanthropus (Chad, Africa, 7 Million Years Old):** Say hello to our early human ancestor! In Chad, scientists found skulls and jawbones that told tales of tiny brains and big adventures. These ancient dudes were probably the first to strut their stuff on two legs!

- **Ardipithecus kadabba (Ethiopia, 5.2 - 5.8 Million Years Old):** Between 1997 and 2004, scientists in Ethiopia discovered fossils of a new human ancestor. These fossils had ape-like features, making us rethink what we know about our earliest family members. It's like finding a hidden level in a video game!

- **Lucy (Ethiopia, 3.2 Million Years Old):** Say hello to Lucy! Found in 1974, Lucy's skeleton was almost complete and showed us that our ancestors could walk upright much earlier than we thought. She's like the rock star of fossils!

- **Neanderthal (Germany, 400,000 Years Old):** In 1856, a Neanderthal fossil was found in Germany. These ancient humans had unique features and were really smart—they even buried their dead! It's like discovering a long-lost branch of our family tree.

- **Jebel Irhoud Fossils (Morocco, 300,000 Years Old):** In 2017, fossils from Morocco blew everyone's minds! They pushed back the timeline for early Homo sapiens, helping us understand more about our origins. It's like finding out the hero's backstory in an epic movie!

- **Omo Remains (Ethiopia, 195,000 - 233,000 Years Old):** Skulls and bones found in Ethiopia gave us clues about the early days of modern humans. These fossils suggested that our species might be older than we thought, adding an exciting twist to our story!

- **Mungo Man (Australia, 42,000 Years Old):** Meet Mungo Man from Australia! His discovery gave us a peek into ancient Aboriginal life and challenged what we thought we knew about their history. It's like uncovering a secret chapter in a book!

- **Tianyuan Man (China, 39,000 - 42,000 Years Old):** Fossils found in China marked some of the earliest evidence of humans in Eurasia. They offer tantalizing clues about our ancient Asian ancestors, making it feel like a global treasure hunt!

- **Cro-Magnon Man (France, 30,000 Years Old):** The Cro-Magnon fossils found in France revealed some of the earliest known Homo sapiens in Europe. These ancient humans were a lot like us, showing that we have more in common with our ancestors than we might think!

Let's Wrap It Up!

So, fellow time travellers, what have we learned today? Fossils aren't just rocks—they're the keys to unlocking Earth's ancient secrets! With a little curiosity and a whole lot of digging, who knows what awesome discoveries await? Keep exploring, keep digging, and never stop uncovering the incredible stories hidden beneath our feet!

Unveiling the Marvels of Muslim Scientists' Contributions!

Fellow explorers of knowledge! Are you ready to board on a thrilling adventure through the ground-breaking ideas of Muslim scientists? Buckle up, because we're about to dive deep into the kingdoms of philosophy, ethics, and evolution!

Meet the Masters of Muslim Thought!

From the bustling streets of Baghdad to the grand libraries of Persia, Muslim scholars blazed trails of wisdom during the Golden Ages. Let's uncover the genius of three remarkable minds:

1. Imam Al-Jahiz: The Zoological Wizard!

Picture this: it's the 9th century, and a brilliant scholar named Al-Jahiz is scribbling away in his study. His masterpiece, "The Book of Animals," isn't just any old encyclopaedia—it's a treasure trove of zoological wonders! Al-Jahiz observed the natural world with a keen eye, noticing how animals adapted to their environments and competed for survival. Little did he know; his ideas would plant the seeds for future theories of evolution!

2. Ibn Miskawayh: The Philosopher!

Fast forward to the 10th century, and we meet Ibn Miskawayh, a Persian philosopher with a mind as sharp as a scimitar! His magnum opus, "The Refinement of Character," delves into the deep waters of ethics and morality. But that's not all—this philosophical powerhouse also dared to ponder the mysteries of evolution. From minerals to humans, Ibn Miskawayh traced the grand tapestry of life with metaphysical finesse!

3. Ibn Khaldun: The Sage of Societies!

Now, let's zoom ahead to the 14th century and meet Ibn Khaldun, the polymath extraordinaire! His masterpiece, "The Introduction," isn't your average history book—it's a sweeping epic that explores the rise and fall of civilizations. But Ibn Khaldun wasn't content with just history—he dipped his toes into the waters of evolution too! From minerals to monkeys, Ibn Khaldun spun a tale of transformation that would intrigue scholars for centuries to come!

Join the Evolutionary Odyssey!

From ancient minerals to the heights of human thought, Muslim scientists paved the way for modern ideas of evolution. While their theories may differ from Darwin's, their contributions to the tapestry of knowledge are nothing short of extraordinary!

Let's Wrap It Up!

So, fellow seekers of wisdom, what have we learned today? Muslim scientists didn't just ponder the mysteries of the universe—they dared to challenge the boundaries of human understanding! With every observation and insight, they carved a path for future generations to follow. Let's raise our hats to these brilliant minds and continue our quest for knowledge, one discovery at a time!

3: Research on Human Evolution

Let's do some Research!

Okay, imagine this: People have different takes on how humans came into existence. Some are all about the idea that God whipped up Adam and Eve straight from scratch, no evolution involved. They're like, "Who needs evolution when you've got divine magic, right?"

But wait, there's more! Some folks think that jumping on the evolution train is a big no-no, like wearing socks with sandals—totally forbidden! This belief has been handed down through the ages by scholars, but here's the twist: it's not exactly written in the Quran.

Now, hold onto your hats, because in the next chapters, we're diving deep into the Quran to reach the truth. We'll decode why so many peeps still cling to the creationism story. And guess what? We're doing it without any preconceived notions, just good old investigating.

The Quran's like a treasure chest full of different types of verses; some crystal clear, others shrouded in mystery like a secret code waiting to be cracked. These cryptic verses are like the breadcrumbs leading to a grand adventure of interpretation. It's like a puzzle waiting to be solved!

Our research zooms in on those mysterious verses. And hey, if you've got a different take on what we find, no sweat! Islam is all about respecting diverse viewpoints, like choosing between pizza or burgers - both tasty in their own way!

So, buckle up and get ready for a wild ride! The Quran says, **"Travel in the world and see how God has originated creation."** It's like a cosmic scavenger hunt, with a twist of divine mystery!

4: Wonderful Beginning of the Life

The Amazing Story of Life

The journey of how life began is super cool! It's like a giant puzzle, and both the Quran and science give us some of the pieces. Let's dive into this awesome adventure!

Imagine you have a magical book that's over 1,400 years old—the Quran. It has talked about the origins of life in many verses. Now, think of scientists as modern-day detectives with cool gadgets, discovering new clues about how life started. When we put the Quran's ancient wisdom and modern science together, we get a clearer and more exciting picture!

Nafs-in Wahid: The Story of a Single Cell

Let's explore the fascinating concept of **Nafs-in Wahid** from the Quran, which talks about the beginning of creation of human beings from a "single cell" or "single living organism." It's like starting a grand building from just one amazing dot!

The Arabic word **Nafs** means living thing and **Wahid** means a single. Combining both words, it means "a single living thing." Imagine life on Earth beginning like a tiny seed that slowly grows into a huge tree.

This idea fits with scientific theories about how life began on Earth. Some scientists believe that life started from a simple cell that divided into two identical cells. This process is called mitosis.

The Quran supports the theory and adds an interesting twist to this story. It talks about creating another cell from the single cell. What's cool is that the Quran doesn't say if the gender of these cells is a boy or a girl. Instead, it uses the word **Zaoj**, meaning spouse or partner. This fits with the idea that figuring out who is a boy and who is a girl came later in the evolution of life and the process is called miosis.

Understanding the World: Science and the Quran

When scientists try to understand the world, they often ask questions like "How does a tree grow from a seed?" or "What makes a rainbow?" The Quran also explores these questions but goes further by asking "why" things happen. It teaches us that God wanted to create humanity from a single cell and then create its partner. According to the Quran, the reason behind everything is that God intended it to happen this way.

This idea in the Quran matches a scientific theory called Abiogenesis. This big word means the study of how life started from non-living things, like how a cake starts from simple ingredients like flour and eggs. Seeing how the Quran and science tell similar stories about the beginning of life is like finding two pieces of a puzzle that fit perfectly together. It's a fun and fascinating way to learn about where we all come from!

Clay: Important ingredient of the Single Cell

Imagine a big, bubbling pot of soup, but instead of in a kitchen, it's under the ocean! These special places, called hydrothermal vents, are like nature's hot springs, but with a twist. They shoot out hot, mineral-filled water that can create something amazing: life!

Some scientists think that these vents could have helped start life on Earth. They believe that the minerals in the water, especially clay, might have mixed with other stuff to make the building blocks of life.

Now, let's dive into what the Quran says about how humans were made. It's like a recipe for creating people! In one verse, it talks about how God began making humans from clay. Another verse compares us to plants, saying we grow from the earth like they do.

The Quran mentions different stages of forming a human from clay, including dust, clay, mud, extract of clay, sticky clay, and hard clay. These stages show the step-by-step process of creating a single cell that eventually becomes a human.

Water: Another important ingredient of the Single Cell

The Quran describes how all creatures, including humans, were made with water. It's like saying we're all made from the same recipe, just with different shapes and sizes. Water is super important because it helps living things grow and stay alive.

But how did humans come to be? Well, the Quran tells us that we started as a single cell, kind of like the tiniest building block of life. Then, we grew and changed, just like how a seed grows into a plant. This process of creation is compared to making things from clay, step by step, until they become solid and real!

Bringing Boys and Girls into the Picture

Now, let's talk about how boys and girls come into the picture. The Quran talks about how God created humans from dust, then from something called Nutfa, which is like a special cell. After that, God made mates, which means boy and girl cells, so they could come together and create more cells. This process is the foundation of how life continues to grow and thrive.

Even though there's still a lot to learn, it's fascinating to see how ancient wisdom and modern science can sometimes come together to tell the story of how life began!

5: Entry of Bashar in Evolution play

Who were Bashar?

Have you ever heard the word **Bashar**? It's like a special word that the Quran often use to describe human beings, but this word does not always refer to us, the humans because the Arabic word for humans is **Insan**. Bashar refers to the earthly, animal side of humans, including our instincts and natural behaviours. It's like saying we're a mix of human and animal!

Imagine if scientists explained how humans evolved from a tiny cell to who we are now. They'd have a long list of stages, but the Quran skips straight to the exciting part: the evolution of Bashar. It's like jumping to the best scenes in a movie and skipping the boring bits!

Now, let's use our imagination: think of Bashar as including all the ancient human-like creatures we find in fossils, except for us, the modern humans that are known as **Homo sapiens sapiens**.

In the next chapter, we'll discover how Bashar turned into human beings. But here's a fun fact: by the end of this journey, only one kind of Bashar species, Homo sapiens, was still around. All the other types, like the **Neanderthals** and

Denisovans, had disappeared from the Earth. Stay tuned for more adventures in the amazing story of how we became who we are today!

Were Apes our ancestors?

Imagine if we could travel back in time and meet our ancient ancestors. Would they look like us, or would they be a bit different? Well, the Quran doesn't give us a clear answer about whether our ancestors were apes. But it does allow us to think about it in an exciting way!

Imagine you're reading a mystery book, and there's a part where the detective doesn't solve the case right away. Instead, they leave some clues for you to figure it out. That's kind of what the Quran does with the question of whether we came from apes. It doesn't say yes or no directly, but it leaves some clues for us to think about.

Now, let's talk about a character from another story: Satan. In the Quran, Satan had a bit of a problem with pride. He thought he was better than humans because he didn't want to bow down to Adam, who was one of the first humans. Satan couldn't see past his own pride, just like some people today might struggle with the idea of being related to apes because they see themselves as superior.

But here's where it gets interesting: In the olden days, some Muslim scholars were already discussing ideas similar to having apes as ancestors! This idea was called the "Mohammadan Theory of Evolution." Isn't that cool? It shows that people have been thinking about these questions for a long time.

According to Islamic rules, something can only be forbidden if it's clearly stated in the Quran or the sayings of Prophet Muhammad. Since the Quran doesn't directly say that humans can't be related to apes, it leaves room for us to explore and learn more about the world through science.

So, next time you think about where we came from, remember that it's like solving a mystery with clues from the Quran and science! It's a big puzzle waiting to be solved, and who knows what exciting discoveries we'll make along the way?

6: Here comes the First Human being

First Human being

Have you ever wondered how the first human was created? Let's dive into an amazing story from the Quran that explains this in a fascinating way.

Bashar: The Pre-human being

A long, long time ago, God decided to create a new kind of being. These beings were called "Bashar". Bashar might sound like a fancy word, but it just means a kind of creature with animal-like instincts, similar to how we sometimes follow our natural habits. For example, humans have natural habits, like feeling hungry and eating food, or feeling tired and sleeping to rest our bodies.

The Magic Moment

Once the Bashar was ready, God breathed a special spirit called **Rooh** into it. The moment the Rooh entered the Bashar, it became a fully developed human being.

A Unique Creation

Humans are special because we're made from both clay and this magical Rooh. This means we have physical bodies like Bashar but also a spiritual side that makes us unique. In the Quran, this is described as created by God's "two hands," which is a way to show that humans are made with extra care and attention.

Prostration of Angels

When the first human was fully created, God told the angels to bow down to this new creation. This human was named **Adam**. The angels bowed down as a sign of respect, but there was one who didn't: Satan. He was too proud and couldn't accept that humans, made from clay, could be so special.

Learning and Growing

The Quran teaches us that while we can learn a lot about our physical world through science (like how plants grow or how stars shine), there are some things, like the Rooh, that are beyond our understanding. These are the magical, spiritual parts of us that make life so mysterious and wonderful.

Reflecting and Understanding

The Quran encourages us to think, explore, and learn about the world around us. It tells us to reflect on how amazing creation is, from the smallest ant to the tallest mountain. And even though we might not understand everything, like the true nature of the Rooh, it's okay. Some things are meant to be magical mysteries that we appreciate and believe in.

What Makes Rooh So Special?

The Rooh is what makes us more than just creatures made of clay. It gives us some super cool abilities:

Spiritual Essence: The Rooh is like a divine gift from God. It connects us to something bigger than ourselves, giving us a higher purpose in life.

Consciousness: With the Rooh, we become aware of ourselves and the world around us. We can think about big questions, like why we're here and what life means.

Emotions: The Rooh gives us feelings. We can feel happy, sad, love, and empathy. These emotions help us form relationships and build a caring world.

Intellect: The Rooh allows us to think and solve problems. It helps us learn, invent, and create amazing things, from stories and music to technology and science.

Metaphysical Connection: The Rooh lets us wonder about the mysteries of life, like the existence of God and the nature of the spirit. It helps us explore the spiritual side of our existence.

From Bashar to Human: A Special Role

When Bashar transformed into a human with the Rooh, God gave humans a very special job. In the Quran, God says to the angels, "I'm going to make a human my representative on Earth." This means humans were chosen to take care of the world and each other.

What Does Being God's Representative Mean?

Free Will: We can make our own choices. We are responsible for our actions and should make good decisions that align with kindness and justice.

Moral Responsibility: We should be fair and compassionate. This means treating everyone with respect and helping those in need.

Spiritual Growth: We should try to grow spiritually by praying, reflecting, and doing good deeds. This helps us stay connected to God.

The Big Picture

Being human means, we have a unique role and purpose. We are like stewards of the Earth, taking care of it and making it a better place. We also have a spiritual side that connects us to God and helps us understand the deeper meanings of life.

7: Adam one of the first Human beings

Adam

Did you know that the name **Adam** means "earth" or "ground" in the old languages of Aramaic and Hebrew? Imagine being named after the ground you walk on! That's because, in the stories from long ago, Adam was created from the soil of the earth.

Adam's Unique Creation

Muslims believe that Adam was the first human being, but there's a twist! The Quran, the holy book of Islam, doesn't say he was the very first person ever. Instead, it tells a story of how early humans, called Bashar, were transformed into real human beings. How? By receiving a special gift from God called a Rooh (Spirit).

So, think of Bashar like characters in a video game who level up to become full humans when they get the special spirit power-up!

The wonderful story of Adam

Picture a game where you whisper a secret message to a friend, who then tells it to another friend, and so on. By the time the message reaches the last friend, it's totally different! That's how the story of Adam changed over time, with each person adding their own imaginative flair.

Let's dive into Quran to see what actual story of Adam is!

Creation of Adam

So, now we know the amazing journey of how Adam was created! It all started from a tiny single cell, the very beginning of life. This tiny cell went through many, many stages of evolution, changing and developing over millions of years, to the stage of Bashar and then transformation of Bashar into a fully developed human being.

God's Order of bowing Adam

Once the Bashar was transformed into a human, something extraordinary happened. God ordered all the angels to bow down to this new creation. And who was representing all humans at that moment? Yes, it was Adam! But someone refused.

Who refused God's order?

So, who refused to bow down to Adam? It was **Azazeel**, who was a Djinn. Djinns are made of smokeless fire, unlike humans who are made from clay. Azazeel was very proud and arrogant. Because of his pride, he thought he was better than Adam.

When Azazeel refused to follow God's order to bow down to Adam, he was given a new name: **Iblis**. We also know him by another name—**Satan**. Iblis said to God, "Adam is made of clay, and I am made of fire. I am better than him, so I will not bow down."

Satan's Punishment

God became very angry with Satan for his arrogance and disobedience. Because of his pride and refusal to follow God's command, Satan was cast out. God told him to go away, marking the beginning of Iblis's role as an enemy to humans.

The big test of Adam and Eve

Satan asked God for time to prove that humans, including Adam, were not worthy of respect. He promised to make Earth so appealing that humans would disobey God.

To warn humans of Satan's trickery, God placed Adam and his wife, **Eve**, in a garden for a special test. In this garden, they could enjoy everything they wanted—except for one tree. God specifically told them not to eat the fruit from this tree.

Tricked by Satan

After some time, Satan began tricking Adam and Eve. He whispered tempting lies, telling them that eating the forbidden fruit would make them immortal. Sadly, Adam and Eve believed him and ate the forbidden fruit.

The Punishment

As a consequence of their disobedience, God instructed Adam and Eve to leave the garden immediately. Ashamed and remorseful, they begged God for forgiveness. God, in His mercy, forgave them but warned them to beware of Satan, their enemy.

Learning from Mistakes

Let's talk about how Adam and Eve reacted after they goofed up. Picture this: Satan, all proud and stubborn, refused to change his mind. But Adam and Eve felt very sorry for what they did. They knew they messed up big time and wanted to fix things with God.

So, what did they do? They didn't make excuses or blame others. Nope! They admitted they were wrong and asked God to forgive them. And you know what? God, being super kind, forgave them right away.

Now, here's the cool part: this teaches us that saying sorry when we mess up and asking for forgiveness is super important. It's like hitting refresh on our friendship with God, making it even stronger than before.

Cool facts about Adam's story

A Unique Leader: Adam was not just any human; he was a leader. Imagine being the first captain of the Earth team!

Learning and Teaching: Adam was taught by God and then he taught others. He was the original teacher of humankind!

Curiosity and Mistakes: Just like how we sometimes get curious and make mistakes, Adam and Eve did too. Their story reminds us that making mistakes is part of human experience.

Fun Thought Experiment

Imagine you're playing a game where you start as a simple character, a Bashar. To become a hero like Adam, you need to find the special Rooh power-up. Once you get it, you level up, gaining special abilities like thinking deeply, understanding right from wrong, and feeling emotions like love and kindness. This transformation makes you ready to take on new challenges, like being a leader and helping others.

By thinking of Adam's story this way, we see that it's about growth, learning, and becoming the best version of ourselves. Just like Adam, we can all strive to be better, learn from our mistakes, and take care of the world around us.

Final Task Guys!

Now that you've learned how humans came to be, here's your last task: teach your family and friends about it! Share the story of the Bashar and the Rooh, and explain how Azazeel refused to bow down to Adam. Have fun being the teacher!

Printed in Great Britain
by Amazon

43346641R00037